Colored

AN ILLUSTRATED STORYBOOK WITH COLORED WOMEN AND THEIR COLORFUL EXPERIENCES OF OVERCOMING OPPOSITION

TEACHIA TURRENTINE

To my baby girl, Ja'el:

The plan for you to win, begins by journeying within.
In this journey, discover anew,
how deeply you are loved, through and through.
As you count both big and small wins,
at the top of the list, should be loving the skin you are in.

You are my favorite, BLACK, BEAUTIFUL, girl.

Love,

Mama

CONTENTS

INTRODUCTION

Wow. What a time to be alive. What a time to be black. This book is birthed from a place in my life where the scales have fallen from my eyes, allowing me to see how much of a privilege and honor it is to be a black, proud, woman. In the face of racism and injustice, I was met with the question, "what can I do to make a difference?" I still don't know that I can answer this question fully, as I believe I am on a journey of revelation regarding the matter; however, the onset of my journey began with me educating myself about my blackness and history. This is when I discovered the term, Colorism, which unraveled another layer of ignorance that I had been comfortably nestled in for far too long. This revelation also exposed to me a greater level of change and impact that is begging to be made. Then, I realized. . . here, on my own front porch, in my own community, with my own people, is where I begin and where I make arguably the greatest impact.

What can we do within our community to educate and empower ourselves in ways that will allow us to infiltrate, represent, and shake the system to its core? The system that was never meant for us to SURVIVE, let along thrive. We stand together. We share our stories. Talk about the hard stuff. Mend relationships. Put aside differences. Support one another, and never give up in our effort to manifest the lives we deserve.

So, here I start by telling the stories of black women, who have experienced hardships stemming from a history and narrative of oppression. Despite these hardships, the stories of these women also sing a song of the relentless conquering of every obstacle meant to keep them bound in the trenches of inferiority, dissatisfaction, and disharmony. As you read these stories and color the pictures, I invite you to reflect upon your own story, as well as the collective stories of black and brown girls and women throughout the nation. In doing this, please consider your part in influencing change. It's time.

With Love,

Leachia Jumentine

1

RELEVANT TERMS

- **Racism:** discrimination or prejudice toward someone of a different race, based on one's idea that their own race is superior to that of other races.
- **Preference:** the basis of liking or desiring something or someone, over something or someone else.
- **Prejudice:** an unfavorable belief, feeling, or opinion, especially toward someone else, without reason, basis, or knowledge.
- **Privilege:** a benefit, honor, or opportunity granted to a particular person or group of people.
- **Colorism:** discrimination or prejudice toward someone of the same race, whose skin is a different shade.
- **Oppression:** extended unjust or cruel treatment, abuse of power, or control, imposed upon a person or people.
- **Liberty:** freedom from oppression and unjust treatment, caused by those with power.
- **Open Mind:** consideration of new ideas, thoughts, and behaviors, that differ from what one is used to; unprejudiced.
- **Revelation:** the discovery of previously unknown facts or ideas.
- **Evolution:** the process of development and growth over time.
- **Demonstration:** the clear and open display or exemplification of a belief or stance.

Colorism

Where to begin?

Let's start at the beginning.

God created all things, but He created human beings in a very special way. . . His image.

Male and female, both created like God and loved deeply by Him.

But after the fall of Adam and Eve, people from all over, gave rise to division through their own selfish and manipulative plans.

This evil intent led to the conception and birth of Colorism.

The thing about Colorism is that it's often subtle, while at other moments, pounces like a roaring lion, seeking to devour.

This atrocity can be traced back to the enslavement of black men, women, and children, that began over 400 years ago. Fair-skinned women were raped and favored by slave owners, which inevitably caused darker-skinned women to develop an inferiority complex.

1

Colorism has hitchhiked on the back of time for centuries, drawing a wedge between black women and black people of all shades, causing competition, and tearing down, instead of collabing, and building up. It has served as another layer in the grander scheme of systemic issues and black oppression, leading to presumptions about the intelligence, appeal, criminal behavior, and overall worth of those with varying levels of melanin. These presumptions have not only been fueled by those of different races and cultures, but those in the black community as well.

As you read the stories and color the pictures of black women throughout this book, allow yourself to experience the feelings that arise, whether good or bad.

Know that your feelings are natural and that allowing yourself to process and navigate through them, will help you become more conscious, receptive, and empowered.

Oppression

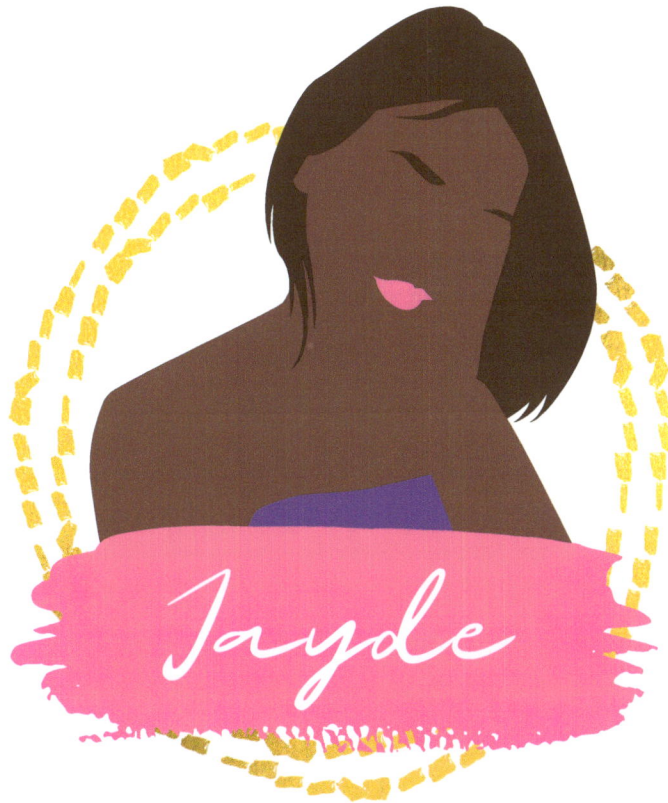

Jayde

Meet Jayde. For most of her life, Jayde has experienced unjust and cruel treatment, due to her darker skin. Growing up, she was told, "you're beautiful, for a chocolate girl," in one breath, and that she would have failed the Brown Paper Bag Test and been a "cotton-picking slave," in the next.

Although the cruel treatment was much more blatant during her younger years, it continued into adulthood, especially in her professional endeavors. Jayde has had to work ten times as hard as her white counterpart, from college, to Corporate America, and still hasn't always gotten what she deserved. She has been rejected for jobs she was overqualified for and been pursued by white men, before cutting ties because their families and friends couldn't get over her being black.

While some of the unjust treatment Jayde has been subjected to, was initiated by those of different races, many of her most traumatizing experiences were at the hands of other black people. Over time, these experiences caused Jayde to, in some ways, believe her back was against the wall. . . that, because of her skin color, something she can't control, she would never be able to get ahead in life. . . then, through a mutual friend, she met Zelda.

Becoming friends with Zelda, has helped Jayde tap into a greater self-confidence and discover a level of persistence that she had not known before . . . persistence that will not allow her to give up, even when treated unfairly.

Liberty

Zelda

Zelda was born a free spirit and given the nickname "Wild One," by her grandmother, because she has always taken risks and played by her own rules. She grew up in a black community that illuminated the many social and racial disparities that black people face every day. Witnessing this, Zelda developed a passion for eradicating injustice and creating equitable opportunities for people of color. The policies Zelda's helped create, the events she's hosted, and the resources she's brought to her community, through activism, have made her a force to be reckoned with; however, her passion has often been expressed in raging and furious ways, at times condoning violence and retaliation, which has gotten her in sticky situations.

Like Jayde, from a young age, Zelda was ostracized by people in her community, because of her fair skin. This caused her to use these incidents as fuel to prove her blackness and sense of belonging.

Zelda's desire to help create equal opportunities for her community, even if partly fueled by her need to prove her belonging, is the very thing that helped Jayde and other women realize that they don't always have to play by everyone else's rules, but can make up their own.

Still, Zelda's contempt toward those who act unjustly and her desire to avenge wrongdoings, sometimes causes her to act irrationally and fails to set the best example for those who look up to her. Her idea of liberty and the right to exercise it however she wants, takes the focus off her positive efforts and causes others to perceive her negatively - the "angry black woman," as some would say - but meeting Kamryn at a peaceful protest, has helped Zelda a great deal.

Getting to know Kamryn, has provided Zelda with a different outlook on life. This relationship has taught her that, having an open mind and practicing peace, does not make her weak; instead, it gives her the ability to be better heard and received by more people, to drive her efforts for change.

6

Open Mind

Kamryn, like so many others, grew up in unstable living conditions. She bounced back and forth, from house to house, and was raised in both predominantly black and white communities. For a while, Kamryn had a hard time figuring out where she belonged because, in the white community, she looked different and her upbringing was different. In the black community, she was made fun of and told that she talked and acted "white."

Kamryn's diverse experiences seemed conflicting to her earlier in life. They caused her to question who she was and become angry with those who labeled her in seemingly derogatory ways; however, later in life, she realized that these experiences helped her to keep an open mind and develop a different perspective on life.

Kamryn's experiences forced her to journey inward to discover who she is in God, and helped her to derive meaning from how these encounters, although not the basis of her identity, helped shape her into the woman she is today.

Frequently journeying inward, allows Kamryn to navigate the world with a sober mind, understanding that, the hate and discord people spew, even when directed toward her, is not because she deserves it or did something to cause it. She knows this behavior often reflects one's ignorance and discontentment with their own life.

Connecting with both Zelda and Sa'de, at the peaceful protest, turned out to be a pivotal moment in Kamryn's life. Both friendships constantly remind her of the need to keep an open mind, and the beauty often revealed through differences.

Revelation

Sa'de

Sa'de lived a mostly unbothered life, until her early adult years. She never thought much about political or social matters, nor did she concern herself with the idea of black oppression. She was so used to breaking through glass ceilings as a young, black woman, that she felt most black people who complained about oppression and inequality, simply weren't willing to take the strides necessary to be successful in life.

Sa'de's thoughts about oppression and injustice changed when she was 23 and witnessed the murder of a black, unarmed, compliant man, at the hands of a white police officer. This incident deconstructed Sa'de's previous beliefs, causing her to realize the dire need for systemic changes.

Sa'de's heart broke as she was faced with the truth that the system, filled with "authority," laws, and politics, was broken . . . that it neither serves nor protects her and her black brothers and sisters, and was never intended to.

Sa'de lay awake every night following the incident, grieved over reality. She faithfully researched history, advocacy, and prayed, asking God what she could do to change the system. . . then, she met Clover.

Sa'de met Clover in a college class. They were the only two black women present and quickly took to one another. Although the two are very different, their friendship developed into a sisterhood authentically. What Sa'de admires most about Clover, is not only her determination and desire to personally evolve, but her bravery in stepping outside of her comfort zone to help others grow, too. Clover helped her see that, to make impactful change, she doesn't have to know all the steps, before taking the first one.

Evolution

Clover

Clover is a product of a family that emphasized the importance of personal growth and evolution. She received so much love and affirmation from her parents, that even when people made comments about the texture of her hair being like a "white girl's," she didn't allow them to stunt her growth. Instead of taking things personally, Clover has used opposition as fuel for continued evolution.

Her goal has always been to focus on her internal world, to create the external reality she desires; however, meeting Justice and seeing that young girls and women of color around her have not always had the same privileges as her, helped Clover develop a passion of advocating for and coaching others, as they develop.

Clover met Justice through her cousin, whom Justice was dating at the time. Initially, she was intimidated by Justice, who had such a radiance and good vibe about her. The more she was around Justice and got to know her, the more she became inspired by her, until finally, she asked Justice to be her mentor. Observing how Justice cares for others and demonstrates it, sparked courage in Clover to dream bigger and do more to serve those she's called to.

Demonstration

Justice

Justice was raised in a community with various pressures, toxicities, and negative influences; from drug dealing, to drug using, murders, abuse, and other crimes. Despite what she witnessed, she always believed that there was a better life available to her. She carried this belief with her throughout her teenage and adult years, and let it be the very thing to motivate her as she navigated through difficult times.

Not only did Justice create the better life she believed was available to her, but through her empowerment organization, she has made it her goal to reach back and demonstrate to others, what is possible in their lives. Justice is very intentional in pouring into others. . . using words to build them up; telling black girls and boys how amazing they are. . . taking an interest in the things that interest others. . . dedicating her time to help her community. . . and standing tall in the face of adversity and injustice. As a result, many have taken to Justice as a mentor and friend and have been inspired to stand up for what's right, to bring about positive change in the world.

Final Remarks

This book tells the stories of colored women with different backgrounds, that have helped shape them into who they are. Individually, these women are powerhouses. . . but together, they are revolutionary and make a far greater impact. Together, they bring their stories of struggle and triumph to the forefront, to create a new story - one filled with learning and growing - true impact. They pull on the strength of one another, formed through their different experiences, and use it as a means of creating a table where they all can sit, and openly welcome others.

So often in our communities, we are enthralled by our own lives and situations, struggles, endeavors, and desires, that we don't always recognize the allies we have in one another. We are better when we are together. That's how we birth a revolution. It starts with us. We must be the change we wish to see.

So, let these individual stories resonate with and inspire you, and allow the colliding of stories to cause a collision in your life, that brings certain change.

We stand together. We represent. We win!

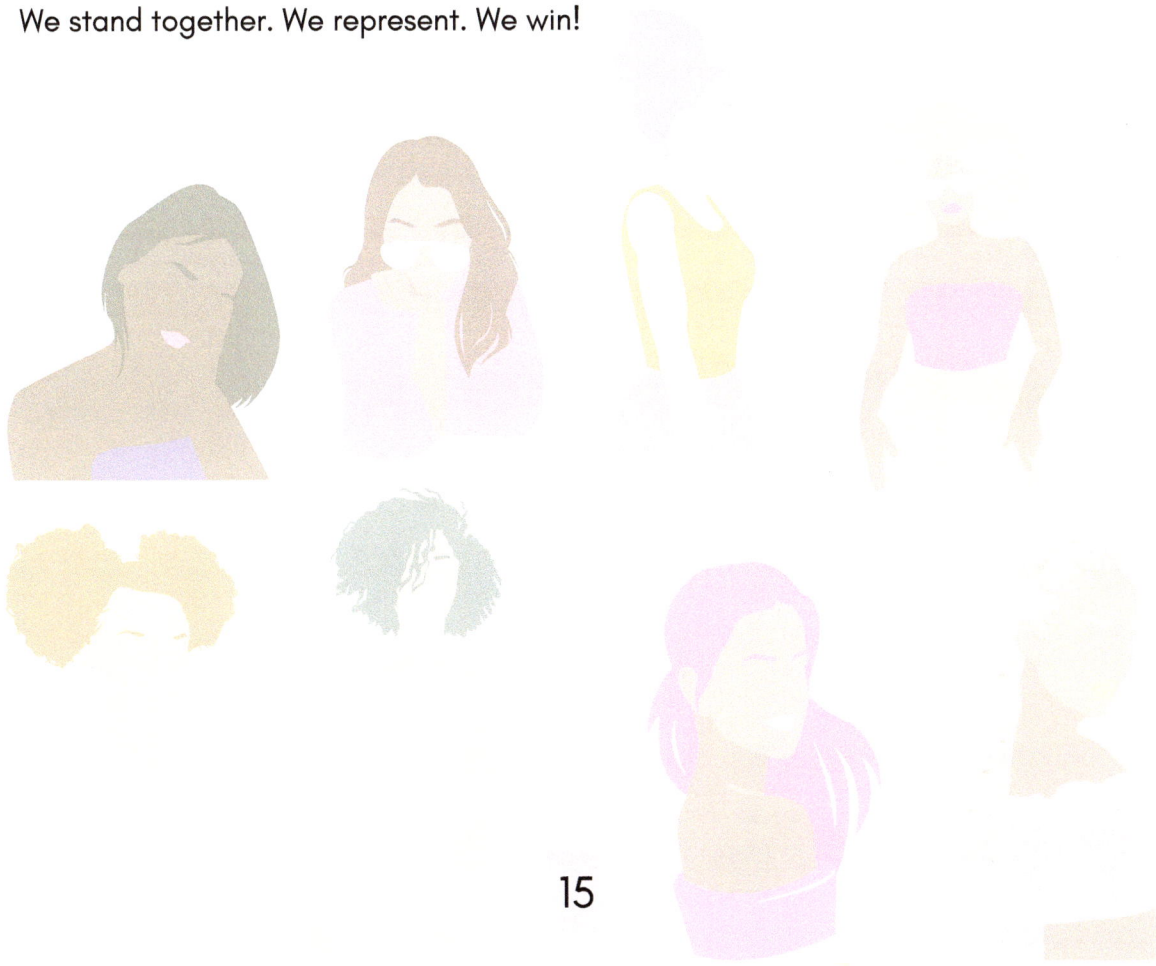

What Now?

To share your story of overcoming opposition as a woman of color, and/or ideas about how to spark real change in our community, please visit the link below:

teachiaturrentine.com/shareyourstory

About the Author

Teachia T.

Teachia Turrentine is a wife, mother, Empowerment Coach, and now two-time author. She is also the founder of BeaUtifully Mended, LLC, an organization that guides women in developing healthy mindsets, to create abundant lifestyles. Teachia is a product of Detroit, with a widely diverse background. From the time she was born, she has faced her share of opposition; however, having discovered her true identity and purpose in God, during early adulthood, Teachia found beauty in her process and has been able to tap into the power that allows her to approach every obstacle, with her head held high. She is committed to creating a different narrative around what it means to be a strong, black, successful woman, which includes helping others along the way. With her story as fuel, Teachia is fully committed to God's plan for her life and knows that her seeds sown, will reap a great harvest for generations to come.

Let's stay connected!

f **BeaUtifully Mended**

⌾ **@teachia.turrentine**

▶ **#TTsJourney**

http:// ⬉ **teachiaturrentine.com**

Share your colored storybook pictures by tagging us and using the hashtags: **#coloredstories #coloredstorybook**

www.ingramcontent.com/pod-product-compliance
Lightning Source LLC
Chambersburg PA
CBHW060854270326
41934CB00002B/139